Tracking the Caribou

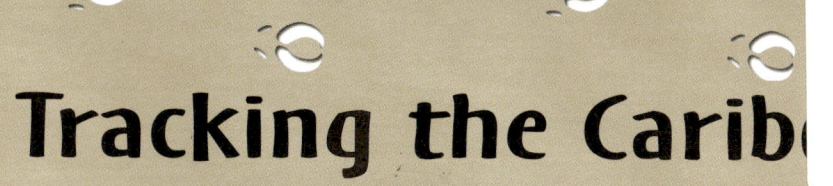

Written by Jane Langford

Contents

The Porcupine Herd	2
Spring migration	4
Summertime	8
Fall migration	10
Tracking the caribou	12
Online tracking	18
Glossary	24

The Porcupine Herd

Caribou are large deer that live in **herds** in Alaska. Alaska is close to the North Pole, so the weather is extremely cold. The caribou have thick, greasy coats to keep them warm in temperatures that often fall as low as -35°C!

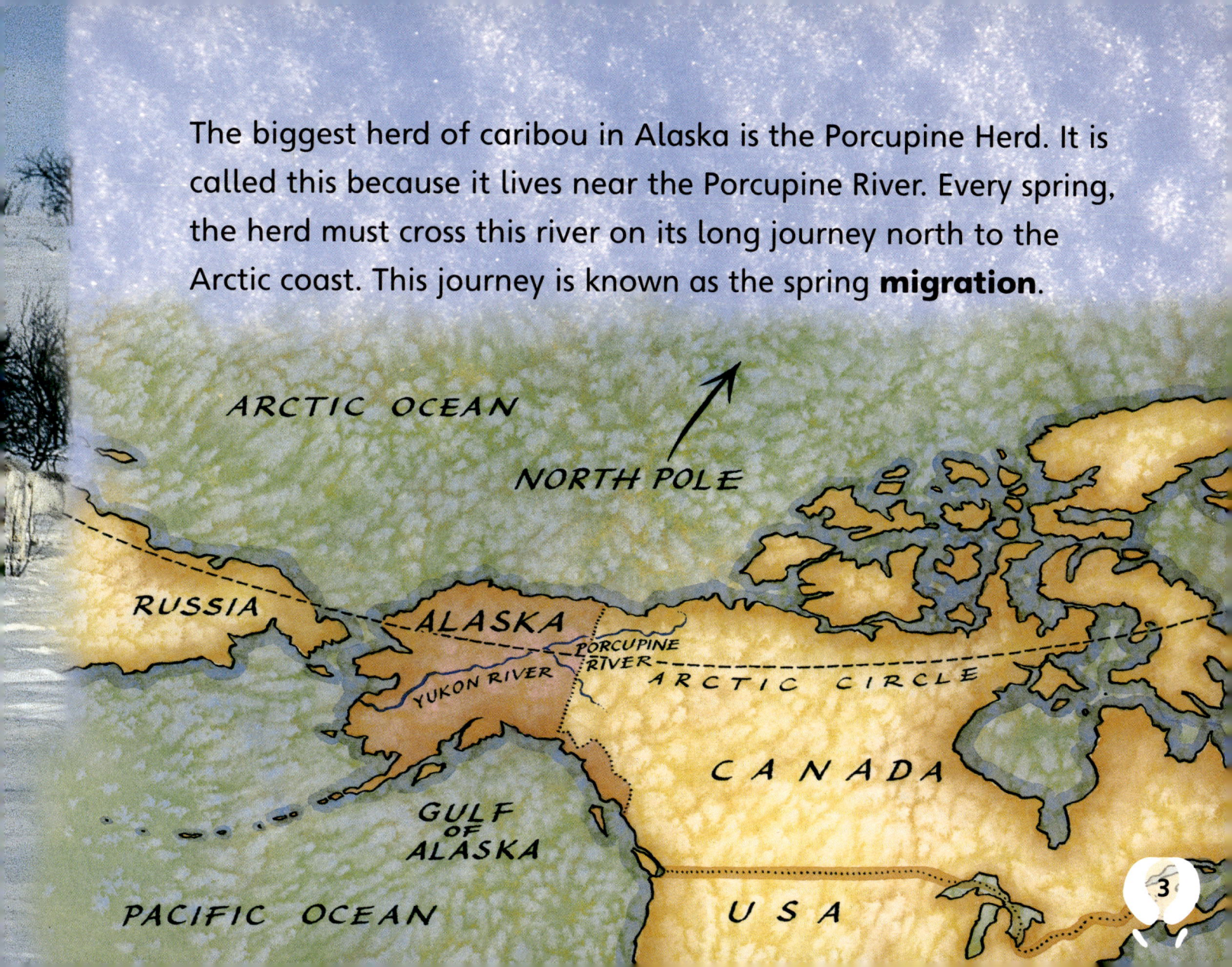

The biggest herd of caribou in Alaska is the Porcupine Herd. It is called this because it lives near the Porcupine River. Every spring, the herd must cross this river on its long journey north to the Arctic coast. This journey is known as the spring **migration**.

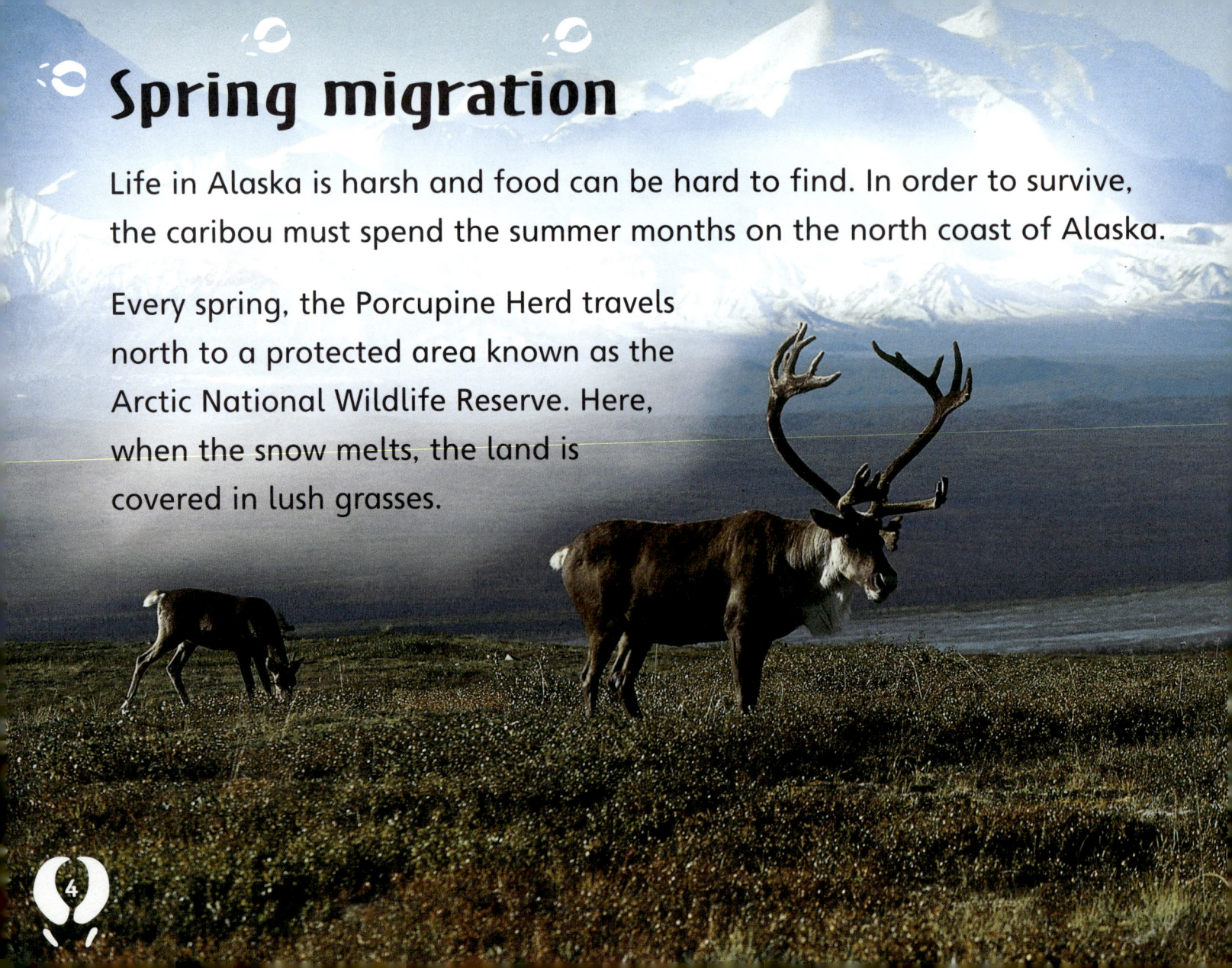

Spring migration

Life in Alaska is harsh and food can be hard to find. In order to survive, the caribou must spend the summer months on the north coast of Alaska.

Every spring, the Porcupine Herd travels north to a protected area known as the Arctic National Wildlife Reserve. Here, when the snow melts, the land is covered in lush grasses.

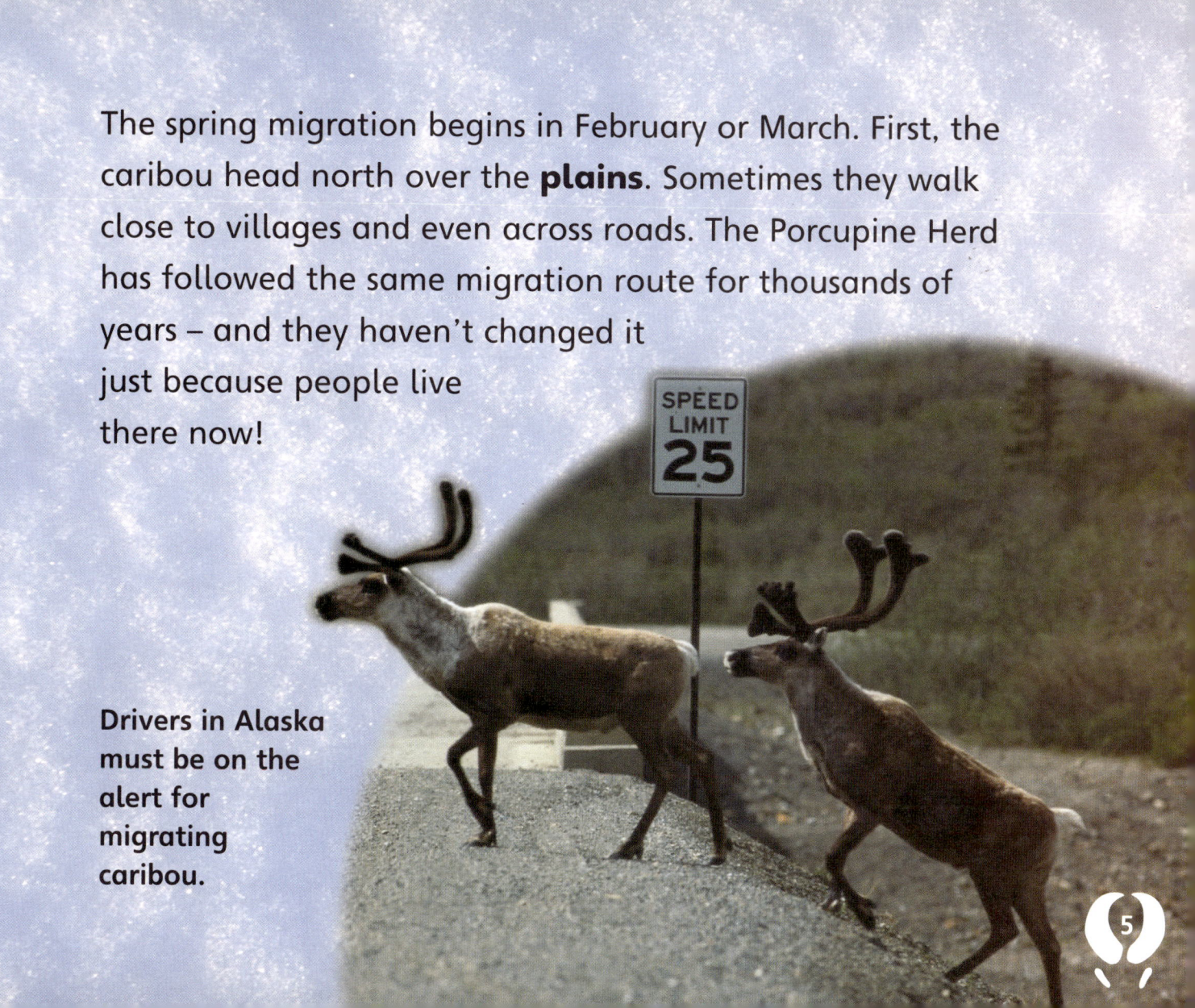

The spring migration begins in February or March. First, the caribou head north over the **plains**. Sometimes they walk close to villages and even across roads. The Porcupine Herd has followed the same migration route for thousands of years – and they haven't changed it just because people live there now!

Drivers in Alaska must be on the alert for migrating caribou.

Next, the herd must cross the Porcupine River. Caribou are strong swimmers. The hollow hair of their winter coats helps them to float in the water.

Once they have crossed the river, the herd travels up through the mountains and valleys of northern Alaska. In May, the caribou finally reach the coast and the safety of the Arctic National Wildlife Reserve.

Summertime

After their long journey, the caribou spend the summer months grazing on the lush grasses. The herd must eat well while the food is plentiful.

In May and June, the female caribou (cows) give birth to their young. The Arctic National Wildlife Reserve is an ideal place for the calves to be born because it is safe from **predators** such as grizzly bears and wolves.

The rich grasses mean that the cows' milk is full of goodness. The calves quickly grow strong enough to make the long journey south in the autumn.

The favourite food of the caribou is cottongrass.

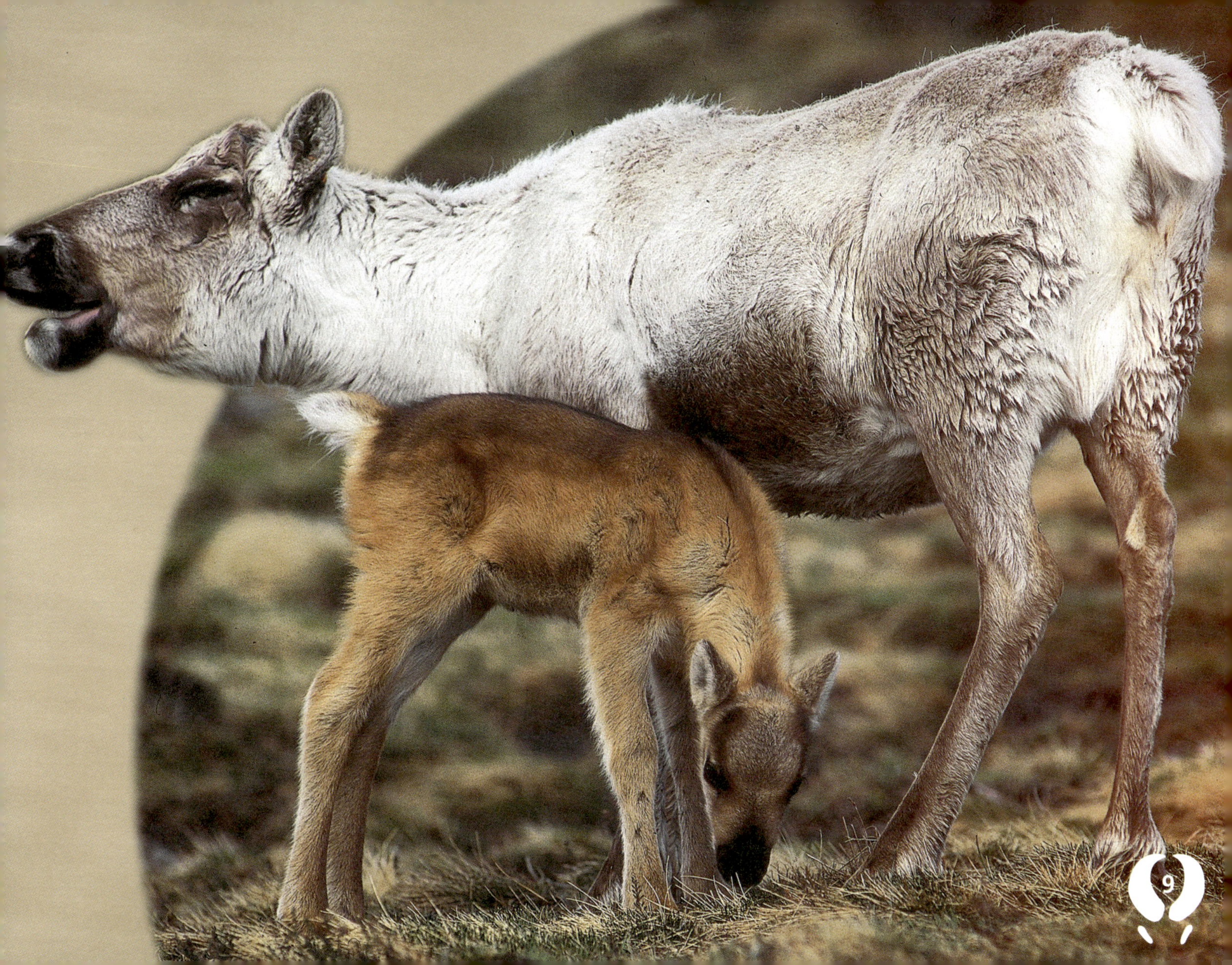

Fall migration

Summer in the Arctic is short. In late July, the north coast becomes bitterly cold and the grasses begin to disappear. The caribou must head back to the southern plains if they are to survive the winter.

The herd begins the **fall** migration in August. It travels south through harsh mountain landscape and back across the icy waters of the Porcupine River.

Finally, the caribou reach their winter home on the southern plains of Alaska. Here the snow is not too deep and they can use their sharp hooves to dig down and find **lichen** and green plants.

When spring comes, they will begin the migration all over again.

The caribou's hoof is a useful tool when looking for food.

Tracking the caribou

Caribou have lived in Alaska for thousands of years. They provide an important source of food, clothing and tools for the local people, the Gwich'in. Gwich'in means 'people of the caribou'.

Scientists, and the Gwich'in people, need to make sure that enough calves are born every year to keep up the numbers of the herd. They also need to know if there are any threats to the caribou during the migrations.

The scientists **track** the caribou as part of a Wildlife Research Project. They want to find out:

- how many caribou arrive safely at the north coast
- how many of the cows give birth to healthy calves
- the exact route of the spring and fall migrations.

These scientists are dedicated to collecting and recording information about the caribou.

How the scientists track the caribou

First, the scientists must catch a few of the caribou (they usually choose cows) and fit collars to them. Each collar contains a **transmitter** that sends a signal up to a **satellite** in space. Once the collars have been fitted, the scientists track the caribou using signals from the satellite.

It takes several scientists to fit the collar to the caribou.

Each time the satellite passes above the caribou, it picks up a signal from the collars. A computer on the satellite works out the position of the caribou. Then it sends this information down to another computer on Earth. The scientists use the information to mark the position of the caribou on a map, and to track the route the caribou herd takes.

signal

satellite

signal

caribou

scientist station

Fitting the collars

In order to fit collars on the caribou, the scientists have to catch them. One way of doing this is from a boat. The scientists wait until the caribou are swimming across a river and then try to capture them. Another way is to fly above the caribou in a helicopter and fire a net over them.

The scientists take great care not to hurt or frighten the caribou when they catch them.

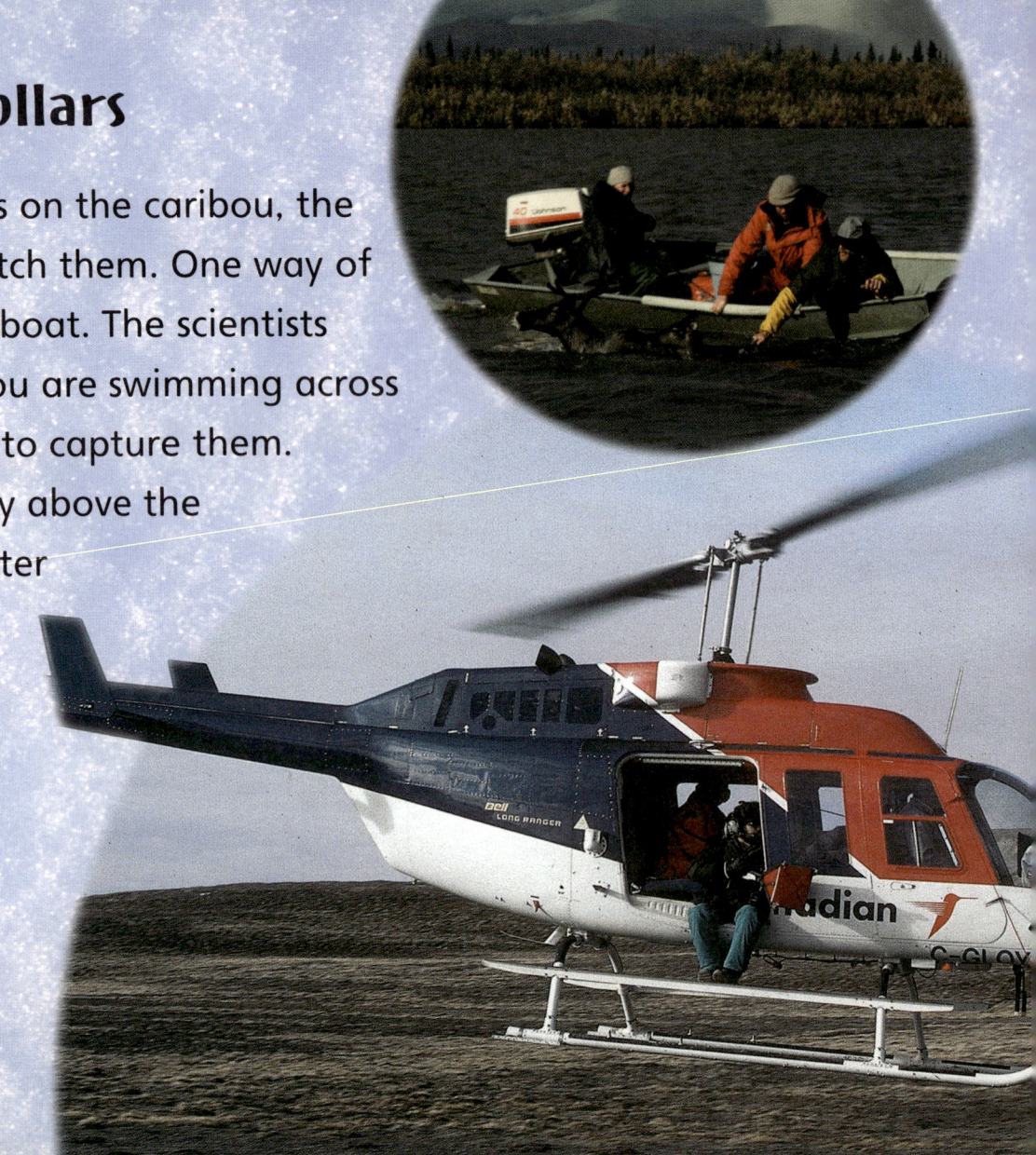

Finding the calves

During the summer, the scientists fly over the caribou herd in an aeroplane. They use the signals from the collars to find the caribou cows. When they identify a collared cow, they look to see if she has a calf.

They count the number of collared cows with calves, and take photographs. All of this information is put on a website.

From mid-air, these scientists are preparing to capture their next caribou.

Online tracking

It is not only the scientists who are interested in the caribou. The caribou-tracking website is very popular with the Gwich'in school children.

The migration route of the Porcupine Herd passes close to the village of Old Crow. The school children at Old Crow have adopted one of the collared cows, and they track her progress using the website.

The scientists update the website with new information every week. The children check the website to see where their cow is. During the summer, the children wait to hear if she has given birth to a healthy calf. The whole school will celebrate when she does!

23

Glossary

fall autumn is known as 'fall' in North America

herd a group of the same animal living together

lichen a plant-like moss, often green or orange

migration a journey made by an animal at a specific time of the year

plains large, flat, open areas of land

predator an animal that kills and eats other animals

track to follow an animal

transmitter a device that passes on a signal

satellite a spacecraft that travels around the earth, picking up and sending out signals

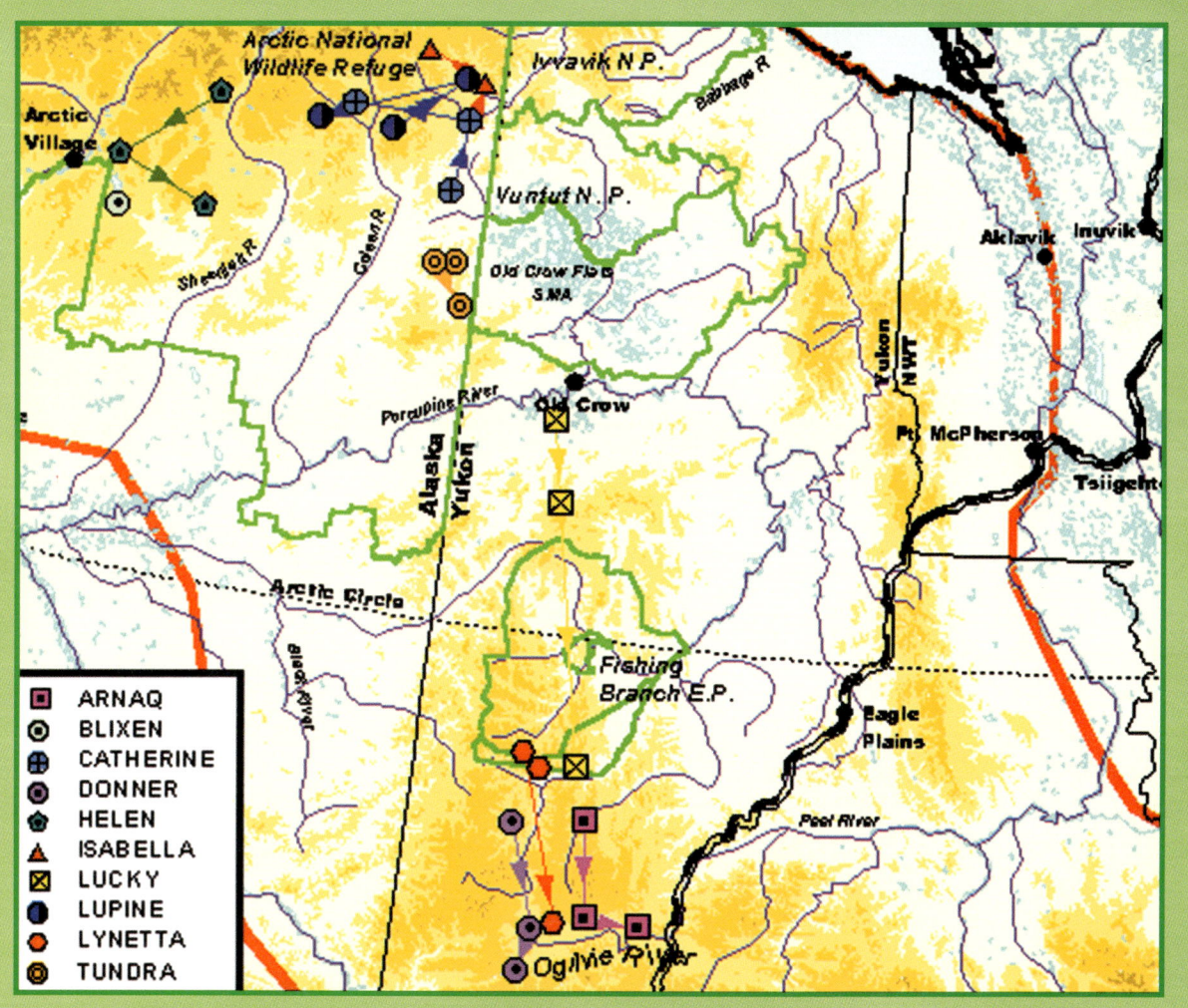

Scientists mark the position of each cow with a different symbol.

Learning about the caribou

When the scientists capture the caribou they don't just fit collars. They measure and weigh each animal, and record the details in a table. All the information they collect is posted on the website.

Name	Donner	Helen	Tundra	Carmen	Arnaq	Lupine
Ptt Id	39842	39841	13314	29684	39769	29752
Capture Date	7-Mar-03	9-Mar-03	10-Mar-03	10-Mar-03	11-Mar-03	13-Mar-03
Capture Time	14:40	13:20	12:35	16:20	16:04	14:00
General Location	Ogilvie River	Whitefish Lakes	Fishing Branch River	Porcupine River	Whitefish Lakes	Blackstone River
Age Class	Medium-Old	Young	Medium	Medium	Young Medium	Young Medium
Calf at Heel?	No	No	Yes	Yes	Yes	Yes
Total Length	197	179	170	188	192	201
Shoulder Height	113	103	107	102	111	109
Chest Height	64	63	64	60	67	65
Hindfoot Length	58	56	56	55	58	56
Metatarsal Length	38	41	39	38	40	38
Neck Circumference	40	42	44	37	46	41
Heart Girth	131	123	129	114	128	113
Body Weight	n/a	92.1	78.9	64.9	99.9 +	76.2

It is not only the children from Old Crow that use the website. Children all over the world can use it to find out about the caribou.

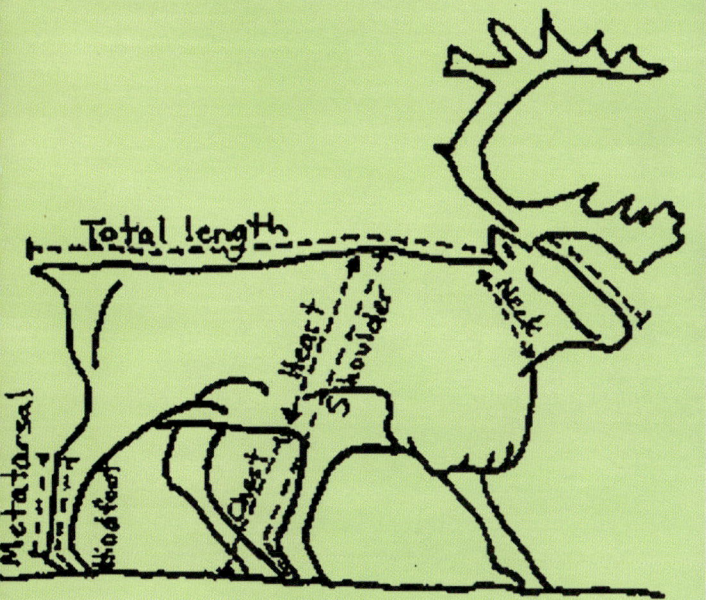

Getting close to the caribou

By tracking the Porcupine Herd's progress on the website, the school children of Old Crow know exactly when the herd are near. Some of the children are lucky enough to actually go and see the caribou. The teachers take them to stay at a camp outside the village.

If they are really lucky, they will see their own special caribou and her new calf.